The
Connell Guide
to

Horatio Nelson

by Roger Knight

Contents

NOTES

Introduction

Horatio Nelson was complex, talented and flawed, possessing great physical courage coupled with enough ambition to last for all of his 47 years. He was driven by a continuous feeling of not being appreciated. Yet at the same time he had an extraordinary professional self-belief: if he thought his way was better he would have no hesitation in breaking rules or conventions; and he generally got away with it.

Long-established, over-simplified myths are the greatest problem faced by a Nelson biographer.[*] Early books focused on Nelson alone, taking little account of those around him and making him a hero who could do no wrong. Victorian writers, often copied later, made out that signs of greatness were obvious from an early age, supporting their view with imagined stories, mostly far-fetched and ridiculous. In fact, there were few signs of exceptional talent in Nelson until the mid-1790s, when he was already in his mid-thirties. Yet this deep veneration continues and his mystique survives to the present day.

The other problem is Nelson's relationship with the remarkable Emma Hamilton. Some newer biographies and television documentaries concentrate on this subject at the expense of his life and achievement at sea. Yet Nelson's private life did not

[*]   Lambert, *Britannia's God of War*, xii

affect his performance or that of the fleets which he led so well. There is one exception, in the summer of 1799 at Naples, when Emma was present and undoubtedly had a damaging influence on his judgement.

Today we are left with icons, symbols and commemorations of Nelson. The name is permanently commemorated in towns: Nelson in the South Island of New Zealand, in Victoria in Australia, in British Columbia and in Lancashire. Perhaps the most famous modern bearer was the young Rolihlahla Mandela, who was called "Nelson" by his missionary teachers in the Transkei when they found his name too difficult to pronounce. Columns supporting a statue of Nelson stand in the middle of London, Edinburgh, Liverpool, Great Yarmouth, and there are statues and plaques in Montreal, Barbados and Simonstown, among other places. Nelson's Pillar also stood in the middle of Dublin, until it was blown up by the I.R.A. in 1966.[*]

Each country and generation has used his memory for its own purpose. In Italy a group of liberal historians in 1889 began to champion the Neapolitan Revolution, claiming that the backwardness of the south of Italy was due to its suppression, and Nelson was cast as the villain.[**] In France, after the fall of Napoleon, the historian Marianne Czisnik notes, Nelson's "genius" and the weakness of French admirals was used to explain

*   MacKenzie, 'Nelson goes Global', 147-161
**   Knight, *Pursuit of Victory*, 543-544

the defeat at Trafalgar. Later in the 19th century, Alphonse de Lamartine and Alexandre Dumas wrote novels stressing the admiral's passion and "blind and fanatical zeal". After surveying French, German and Spanish literature, Czisnik comments: "Foreign perceptions of Nelson have been shaped more by the needs of those societies than by the reality of what Nelson had in fact achieved."[*]

In Britain in the years leading up to the First World War, the Navy League, lobbying for further rearmament against the new threat from Germany, invoked his name. Trafalgar centenary celebrations in 1905 took place all over the Anglophone world. In 1941, during the Second World War, Alexander Korda made the only film of Nelson's life of any distinction called *That Hamilton Woman*. It starred Laurence Olivier and Vivien Leigh and not only told the story of Nelson and Emma, but showed Nelson resisting tyranny in the form of Napoleon: audiences equated the emperor in the film with Hitler. Churchill was reputed to have said that the film was worth two divisions.

In 2005, the bicentenary of Trafalgar was marked by books, conferences and television programmes, while a review of over a hundred warships took place at Spithead: 27 foreign navies sent 52 ships; the French, with great style, sent six, including their largest aircraft carrier, which dominated the view of the warships down the

[*]   Czisnik, *Controversial Hero*, 147-148, 157

Solent.[*] Predictably the review was criticised by the left-wing press, for being held at all, and by the right-wing press, for not doing enough. Controversy aside, the navies of the United States, Russia, China and Japan, all present at the commemoration, still study his leadership and tactics.[**]

This short book seeks a dispassionate view of the man, which can be gained from the thousands of documents which Nelson and those around him left to us in dispatches, reports, letters and logs. It also considers the other parts of the equation: the navy, a formidable organisation of thousands of officers, seamen, administrators and shipbuilders on which Nelson's success depended; and the backdrop of the intense ideological struggle between Britain and France which developed from the French Revolutionary War through the rise of Napoleon into a contest for domination of Europe.

How did Nelson achieve such rapid promotion?

Horace Nelson, as he was called as a child, was born on 29th September 1758 in Burnham Thorpe, a large village in Norfolk where his father, Edmund, was rector. His mother, Catherine (*née* Suckling), was the great-niece of Sir Robert Walpole, the first

[*] Connelly, 'Trafalgar and Popular Culture', 87-97
[**] Hattendorf, 'Nelson Afloat', 182-186

Prime Minister, and it was her side of the family which gave Nelson political and naval connections which enabled him to start in the navy. However, she died when Horace was nine, leaving a large family to be brought up by the unworldly Edmund Nelson. Horace had two older brothers, Maurice and William, who played a large part in his career. They were dull, quite unlike him. Indeed, no other member of the Nelson family, before or since, ever remotely matched Nelson's qualities.

Nelson's one unusually powerful attribute, his capacity to communicate and empathise with his officers and seamen, was perhaps due to his early

THE ROYAL NAVY IN THE FRENCH REVOLUTIONARY WAR?

The Royal Navy achieved some real advantages over the French navy by the time the French Revolutionary War started in 1793, and its superiority continued. In the ten years of peace after the American Revolutionary War had finished in 1783, William Pitt's government had raised extra money, reduced the naval debt and invested heavily in the infrastructure of the navy. New warships came down the slipways. Procedures in the Navy Board and working practices in the dockyards were reformed. Docks at Portsmouth and Plymouth were enlarged and renewed, a huge rope laying building was constructed at Chatham, and many storehouses constructed.

By the mid 1780s, the biggest problem of all was also solved. At the beginning of the American War the fleet had been hastily sheathed with copper, which kept ships' bottoms clear of weed and enabled them to sail faster, life in the country. Burnham Thorpe had a population of 300, with a market every week. The rector's son was in contact with all manner of men and women, from the gentry to the labouring poor. Later in life, only royalty was to prove immune to Nelson's charm. George III did not like him, his naval son Prince William Henry twisted him round his little finger in the West Indies in the 1780s, and the Queen of Naples duped him in 1798 and 1799.

Just before his 13th birthday, on 24th April 1771, Horatio Nelson joined his uncle's ship as a midshipman. The 64-gun *Raisonable* was anchored in the Thames Estuary, hurriedly assembling a crew,

while it also protected the hull against shipworm. However, it was found that the great iron bolts which held the ships together were slowly destroyed by the process of electrolysis, caused by the proximity of copper in sea water. In the mid 1780s a copper alloy bolt was invented which neutralised this process. The huge task of rebolting the entire fleet had to be undertaken, but it was largely achieved by the time that war was declared.

The Ordnance Department tested the entire stock of British naval guns and over half were condemned. New ones were manufactured to a better design. The mixing of gunpowder improved. The light, short-range carronades, perfected at the end of the American War, were produced in quantity and became a crucial feature of Nelson's battle tactics.

In contrast, the French navy was battered by disaster after disaster. In 1783 the battleships of the combined Bourbon powers of France and Spain had outnumbered those of the British, but the financial effort to retain this advantage was one of the chief reasons why the French treasury ran out of money in the late 1780s. A further failure was the huge taking on stores, adjusting her rigging and bending on sails, making ready to go to sea. Britain was in dispute with Spain over the Falkland Islands and the fleet was mobilising to back up the British government's diplomatic pressure.

The captain of the ship, Maurice Suckling, Nelson's mother's brother, was the first in a succession of patrons who supported Nelson through his early career. At this time the captain could decide which officers he took to sea, though they received their commissions from the Board of the Admiralty. It was therefore essential for the family of an aspiring young naval officer to find a patron.

---

and costly project to build a harbour at Cherbourg, which would have transformed the strategic situation in the Channel. But the newly-constructed piers were swept away by winter gales. Money was so tight that French seamen and dockyard workers were unpaid, which in turn led to strikes, contributing to domestic strife which led to revolution. This in turn led to some of the best officers being dismissed from the service. In 1793 the French navy thus had unprepared ships and mutinous crews.

Throughout the French Revolutionary War, British warships were therefore better maintained and more efficient. Their guns were more robust and accurate, because of better gunpowder, while many ships were equipped with gunlocks rather than slow matches, enabling the gunners to aim effectively. Superior copper sheathing made the ships faster. Ships continuously on blockade resulted in highly trained seamen, while French seamen and ships languished in harbour. Nelson's success in battle should be understood with this mind.* ∎

*Knight, *Britain against Napoleon,* 29-45; *Pursuit of Victory,* 131-141

Captain Horatio Nelson, 1781, by J.F. Rigaud

In turn, it was useful for the captain to have a group of young men whom he could train and trust. It was in no one's interests to appoint and promote a young man who did not like life at sea, or who had no aptitude for it.

In 1775 Suckling would become an important administrator, Comptroller of the Navy Board, which enabled him always to be on hand in London to help Nelson's career. He had already used his influence to obtain a berth for Nelson in the *Carcass*, which went on a voyage of exploration to the Arctic during the summer of 1773. Following this, the young midshipman sailed to India and the Arabian Gulf for three years.

He came back very ill, probably suffering from

malaria, but his return was fortuitous. The first shots had been fired in what became the American Revolutionary War and many warships were being commissioned. He recovered quickly, and Suckling managed to get him a berth in the winter of 1775/6 on a short convoying voyage down to Gibraltar and back, to prepare him for the lieutenant's exam which would enable him to stand watch on his own. Nelson had already gained an extraordinary amount of experience, having sailed 45,000 miles, and he passed as lieutenant on 9th April 1777.

The next day Nelson received his commission as second lieutenant of the *Lowestoffe*, a fast frigate of 32 guns captained by William Locker, and set off to the West Indies. Of all those who interested themselves in Nelson's career, Locker was the most influential. He had had a brilliant early career in the Seven Years War. In the West Indies Nelson caught the eye of Admiral Peter Parker, commander in chief of the Jamaica station. After six months as third lieutenant in Parker's flagship Nelson was appointed on 1st January 1779 to his first independent command, a small brig called the *Badger*, in which he distinguished himself and took a prize.

It was not long before the next promotion. On 1st September 1779 Nelson reached the rank of post-captain (that is, appointed to command a 6th rate warship or above) when he was appointed to the *Hinchinbrook* in the West Indies by Parker, only eight years after he had joined the navy as a midshipman. He was just under 21. While he was clearly keen, and had impressed his senior officers, he had not yet displayed any exceptional qualities. The underlying reason for Nelson's rapid rise in the service was that the war in the West Indies was taking its toll on the navy and plenty of vacancies arose for promotion for a young and active officer. Nelson was in the right place at the right time.

When did Nelson first show he was an exceptional commander?

For more than a dozen years after his early promotion to post-captain, Nelson's upward path in the navy stalled. For a start, he became seriously ill, catching a tropical fever in April 1780 when ashore in an expedition against a Spanish fort in central America. He was taken back to England, but another nine months were needed before he was sufficiently recovered for active service. It was not until August 1781 that he commissioned the *Albemarle*, a 28-gun frigate, cruising to the St Lawrence in Canada, New York and the West Indies.

In New York he met two naval officers who would have an effect on his career, neither of them positively, though initially relations were warm. The first was Rear-Admiral Sir Samuel Hood, whom Nelson impressed; the other was a midshipman,

Prince William Henry, the third son of George III, who was equally taken with the 26-year-old naval officer. But in all, it was an undistinguished cruise and not a good time for the navy, with the loss of the American colonies following the American War of Independence and the consequent loss of morale and prestige.

With the peace, Nelson was put on half pay. He set himself the task of learning French, potentially useful for his career, but he signally failed to master the language during his six-month stay in northern France. In March 1784 he received a mark of favour by a peacetime appointment to the *Boreas*, another 28-gun frigate, which was to cruise in the Leeward Islands. This three-year cruise was something of a disaster, and nearly wrecked his career.

The first problem erupted because of a dispute with the West Indian planters, who had long traded with the American colonies in American vessels, but who were now prohibited from doing so by an order of 1783. This permitted trade only in British vessels, owned and built in Britain with British crews. This was an inconvenient piece of legislation, enacted before the signing of the peace treaty between Britain and the United States. It was habitually ignored by planters and merchants, but from Nelson's arrival in the West Indies in November 1784 he was determined to enforce it. He boarded American vessels and sent them to the vice-admiralty courts as prizes, but was challenged repeatedly in the courts by the local planters. After many months, Nelson succeeded in shaming the British government into defending him in the courts. Nonetheless it was a stressful episode, perhaps ill-judged on Nelson's part. With hindsight it was the first sign of an independence of mind: but it also marked the start of his reputation as an intemperate captain who could not be trusted. Worse was to follow.

When the senior naval officer of the Leeward Island station went home, Nelson was left as the acting senior officer. He was then faced with a problem which he handled with astonishing naivety. The *Perseus*, a frigate of the same size as the *Boreas*, arrived on the station, commanded by the 20-year-old Prince William Henry, now grossly over-promoted through the influence of his father. He ran his ship in the only way he knew, with an iron and wilful discipline. He had also fallen out badly with an older first lieutenant, Isaac Schomberg, who had been appointed to assist the inexperienced Prince. Rather than attempting to diffuse this difficult situation, Nelson took the Prince's side and did not keep the Admiralty informed.

After months of poisonous relations aboard the *Perseus*, Schomberg finally requested a court martial and Nelson was persuaded by the Prince that the *Perseus* should sail for Jamaica so that the court martial could take place. The commander-in-chief of the Jamaica station wisely dissuaded Schomberg from proceeding with the court martial.

Had it gone ahead it would have been the end of the careers of both the naval officers involved, and of Captain Nelson's. No naval officer should let personal relations damage the effectiveness of warships on his station. Nelson had antagonised the Board of Admiralty. It seemed clear that he could not be trusted with independent responsibilities.

He was punished by having to spend five years ashore on half pay in Norfolk, and was ignored when the navy was mobilised in 1790 and 1791 to counter the threat of possible war with Spain. Lord Hood, now on the Admiralty Board, made his displeasure well known. Only the declaration of war against Revolutionary France in 1793 saved Nelson's career. With as many ships as possible being commissioned, this was a time for the Admiralty to take risks. Captain Nelson had proved that he was no peacetime commander, but in a war against an aggressive French nation, he just might do well. On 6th January 1793 he was appointed to the 64-gun *Agamemnon*, and was to go to the Mediterranean with Lord Hood as commander-in-chief.

Here Nelson distinguished himself ashore in the successful operations to take Corsica from the French, in the process regaining Hood's respect (though also losing the sight of his right eye). He was frustrated under the next commander-in-chief, the lackadaisical William Hotham, soon replaced by Admiral Sir John Jervis, who reached the

Mediterranean in December 1795. This gritty and aggressive admiral immediately shook up the discipline of the fleet which had become lax. Jervis saw the talent and ambition in Nelson and supported him, gave him responsibility, and ensured that he was given the most junior flag rank, that of commodore. Their relationship dominated the British effort in the Mediterranean for the next four years.

Nelson's potential was at last recognised by a senior admiral. His new-found maturity is best illustrated by a serious but little known incident in January 1797. It was a critical moment. The British cabinet had decided that the British fleet should abandon the Mediterranean. Nelson had transferred his commodore's broad pennant from the 74-gun *Captain* to the large frigate *La Minerve,* and had been sent to bring a convoy of troops to Gibraltar from Porto Ferrajo, the port at Elba, a long way away from the main body of the fleet.

At Porto Ferrajo a serious mutiny blew up in the frigate *Blanche.* Mutiny could often be diffused by negotiation, but this one was dangerous. The *Blanche* had been an unhappy ship with her crew confused and disturbed. Their captain had just been dismissed from the service for sodomy and his replacement, Captain Henry Hotham, had a reputation for extreme discipline. The crew, turning their guns on their officers, was determined not to have him aboard.

A dramatic scene was played out in the

amphitheatre that is Porto Ferrajo harbour, watched by the crews of the other British ships anchored there. First, Nelson sent a lieutenant on board the *Blanche* to call upon the crew to end the mutiny, with the threat of hanging every third man if they did not put down their arms. The crew remained hostile and the lieutenant returned hastily to Nelson on board *La Minerve*. With theatrical timing, Nelson then waited for half an

---

NELSON'S MARRIAGE TO FRANCES NISBET

Intertwined with the many stresses that Nelson experienced when he commanded the *Boreas* in the Leeward Islands was his courtship of Frances Nisbet. She was the niece of a rich planter on the island of Nevis, John Herbert, and the widow of a doctor, Josiah Nisbet. She had a son, also Josiah, who was five when Nelson and Frances met in 1785. They married on 11th March 1787 on Nevis, and Prince William Henry was the best man just before he left the Leeward Island station

precipitately. According to the prince, Frances was a "pretty and sensible woman". In an unusually critical comment, historian Andrew Lambert wrote in 2004, that Nelson's decision to marry was a "foolish and immature decision". *

Their marriage took place just before Nelson and Fanny – she was always called Fanny – sailed to England, after which Nelson spent five years on half pay. They lived in Burnham Thorpe with Nelson's father, Edmund. To have exchanged the comfortable existence as a member of the elite of Nevis for the cold rectory in north Norfolk cannot have been easy. Nor were expectations of a substantial inheritance from John Herbert well-founded.

In the early years theirs was a solid marriage, though

hour, during which the *Blanche's* crew became uneasy. He then came aboard, listened to their grievances, and with a few words won them over. According to one eyewitness, Nelson said: "If Captain Hotham ill treats you, give me a letter and I will support you. Immediately there was three cheers given and Captain Hotham shed tears and Nelson went on board his ship." Very few officers could have emerged successfully from such a

childless, and there was a particular friendship between Fanny and her father-in-law. When Nelson went to sea in 1793, her letters to him reveal her as nervous and anxious, looking for a quiet life, with none of the ambitions which were developing in Nelson. A particular difficulty was his stepson, Josiah, who went to sea, but was thoroughly unsuited to naval life and was a constant disappointment to Nelson, who tried to exert his influence on the young man's behalf.

The social and professional pressures on Nelson in late 1798 and 1799 in Palermo and Naples after the Battle of the Nile changed everything. In such circumstances, the reassurance that the passionate and capable Emma Hamilton

was able to give him drew him to her, and he did not return to England for two years. The final break with Fanny came in January 1801 before he went off to Copenhagen: they never saw each other again. The separation was sealed with the birth of Emma's child Horatia at the end of that month.

Nelson provided for Fanny generously. When they separated, he settled an allowance of £1,600 a year on her and in his will provided her with an annuity of £1,000 a year. But his personal relations with her after his decision to leave were without sentiment, even savage, most likely inflamed by Emma's passionate nature and hatred of her rival. ∎

*Lambert, *Britannia's God of War*, 183

serious situation. However clumsy his relations with princes, he had the rare ability to speak to many levels of society.[*]

What risks did Nelson take at the Battle of Cape St Vincent?

Nelson arrived back at the fleet off Cadiz in *La Minerve*, immediately reported to Admiral Jervis, and transferred his commodore's flag back to his ship of the line, the *Captain* (74). The Spanish fleet was at sea, having convoyed four ships out into the Atlantic on a voyage to Spanish America, where their precious cargo of mercury was needed to convert silver into coin. So desperate was the Spanish government for money that it was taking no chances and provided the ships with a huge escort of 23 ships of the line, one of 130 guns and six of 112 guns, together with 12 frigates. The Spanish were returning to Cadiz and were not seeking battle. Furthermore, they did not anticipate meeting Jervis's fleet, and did not know that he had very recently been reinforced with the addition of five ships of the line.

The morning of 14th February 1797 was misty,

[*] Rodger, 'Nelson and the British Navy', 10-11; Knight, *Pursuit of Victory*, 213-215

with light winds. For the British this was a golden opportunity and it was imperative that the Spanish ships should not escape. The English fleet was heavily outnumbered, with 15 ships of the line, two of 100 guns, and four frigates, but Jervis had been observing the Spanish navy for two years and knew that it was deficient both in the number and quality of its seamen. As the lines of the two fleets approached each other out of the mist, the Spanish commander was caught unawares. Jervis took a calculated risk that superior English discipline and gunnery would outweigh Spanish numbers and steered for them. He signalled to Admiral Sir Charles Thompson, his second-in-command, for his division to tack, but, for whatever reason, this signal was not obeyed.

Nelson realised that unless he took prompt action, the Spanish fleet would escape, and, without direct orders, moved the *Captain* out of the line. Because of the light wind, the *Captain*'s progress was slow, but she approached the division of huge Spanish ships and was soon surrounded by them. This manoeuvre gave the rest of the British fleet time to bring the rest of the Spaniards to battle.

Nelson's decision was physically brave, but he knew that the *Captain*'s superior gunnery would even the odds. The *Captain* was soon supported by Collingwood in the *Excellent,* who followed Nelson out of the line. Collingwood steered the *Excellent* between Nelson and the Spaniards, giving the *Captain* ten minutes respite to make running repairs to rigging and replenish ammunition. Collingwood wrote to congratulate Nelson after the battle: "It adds very much to the satisfaction I had in thumping the Spaniards that I relieved you a little."[*] Some officers complained to Jervis later that Nelson should have been disciplined for disobeying orders; Jervis dismissed the protest.

In the mid-afternoon, amid the great pall of smoke which hung in the nearly-still air, Nelson took another unorthodox and brave decision. The *Captain* was very close to a large Spanish warship, the *San José*, which had in turn collided with the *San Nicolas*, and the rigging of the two ships had become entangled. Both of these ships had had a pounding and Nelson took an instant decision to capture the *San Nicolas* by boarding her, and the *Captain* was made fast to her. It was at this point that a commodore should have ordered a more junior officer to lead the boarding party. But again Nelson broke the rules decisively and boarded the *San Nicolas* himself. (Before this, the last English flag-officer to lead a boarding party in person was probably Sir Edward Howard in 1513.)[**]

It was the Nelson trademark of direct assault. Most of *Captain*'s casualties occurred in these few minutes, at point blank range. A soldier smashed the windows of the *San Nicolas*'s stern cabin, high above the *Captain*'s deck and Nelson leapt through after him. With Nelson protected by his boat crew,

*   Knight, *Pursuit of Victory*, 227
**   Rodger, *Command of the Ocean*, 439

the boarding party rushed the demoralised Spaniards, then went on to overwhelm the *San José*. Both ships surrendered to him. It was an extraordinary few minutes.

In the tough, five-hour battle the *Captain* suffered 80 dead and wounded out of a total of 300 English casualties. Four Spanish warships were taken and about 1,500 Spanish seamen were killed or wounded. The *Captain*'s fire had been devastating. Her gunner recorded that the ship had used 146 barrels of gunpowder, 2,773 cannon shots and 1,940 musket and pistol shots.[*]

Such were the jealousies among the officers in Jervis's fleet that Nelson took especial care that his version of the battle reached the First Lord of the Admiralty, Lord Spencer, and this was the version which the Admiralty made public. For the first time, he became famous. Newspapers extolled "Nelson's Patent Bridge for boarding First Rates". He was promoted to rear-admiral and knighted.

Spurred on by the praise and the accolades, Nelson took one risk too many. Later that summer, he and Jervis (now elevated to the peerage as Lord St Vincent) decided on a surprise attack on the Spanish island of Tenerife to capture a Spanish ship, supposedly full of gold. Nelson took a number of ships south, but the expedition went very wrong. He lost all the advantages of surprise. On the second attack on 25th July 1797 he was wounded in

[*]   Knight, *Pursuit of Victory*, 226

the right arm which had to be amputated. Overconfidence had led to loss of judgement. He returned to England for a painful and depressing period of recuperation and doubts as to whether he would be employed again, though Lord Spencer had no hesitation in sending him back to sea. Thus a one-eyed, one-armed admiral became even more distinctive in the public mind: and he was about to become a legend.

Why was his victory at the Battle of the Nile so important?

On 29th March 1798 Nelson hoisted his flag aboard the 74-gun *Vanguard* and sailed to join Lord St Vincent's fleet off Cadiz. The war was going badly for Britain and her allies. The young French general Napoleon Bonaparte had reinvigorated the French army, now dominant in Northern Italy. French territory had been extended. Austria had made peace with France and was out of the war. Furthermore, intelligence was reaching London of a great expedition of warships, storeships and troop transports preparing in Toulon and other French Mediterranean ports, although no firm information was available as to its destination: Ireland, Portugal or southern Italy were suspected. To counter this threat, the British cabinet sent ten ships of the line from the Channel fleet south to St Vincent, who was still blockading Cadiz with his fleet. The extra ten ships made possible a British presence in the Mediterranean again, after more than a year's absence.

Napoleon commanded an enormous expedition which left Toulon on 19th May. The 15 ships of the line were not well manned and some were very old, but they escorted 280 transports, carrying 48,662 troops.[*] Because of its great size, the cumbersome convoy made its way south slowly, reaching Malta, which surrendered to the French, on 12th June.

On 3rd May St Vincent had sent Nelson scouting into the Mediterranean with three 74-gun ships to gain intelligence of the French, and he was joined by a further ten ships, almost all captained by young, aggressive and talented officers: it made for a highly efficient squadron. For nearly three months, from mid-May 1798, they searched the Mediterranean, but could not find the French. By slow deduction and interpreting local information, Nelson realised that the French had sailed east and he conferred with his senior captains. He outlined the options to them and noted them down on a single sheet of paper, which survives: the last option reads: "Should the Armament be gone to Alexandria and get safe there our possessions in India are probably lost. Do you think we had better push for that place?"[**] It was

[*]   Knight, *Pursuit of Victory*, 279
[**]   National Maritime Museum, Croker Collection, CRK/14

a risky decision: but he chose correctly.

His fast-sailing squadron overtook the slow-moving French expedition which hugged the coast of Crete before it turned south for Egypt. When Nelson reached Alexandria on 29th June there was no sign of the French, and he headed north towards Turkey. He had missed them by a matter of hours. On 1st July Napoleon's army landed at Alexandria, the Egyptians put up no resistance and the French fleet went to anchor in Aboukir Bay, to the east of Alexandria. Three weeks later the French defeated the Egyptian army at the battle of the Pyramids.

A month later, after resting and re-provisioning at Syracuse in Sicily, Nelson's squadron returned to Alexandria and found the French fleet anchored

CUTHBERT COLLINGWOOD

Cuthbert Collingwood (1748-1810) was one of Nelson's earliest and closest friends, and a completely different character: shy, cautious, thoughtful. The two young midshipmen met in 1773 at Sheerness when they were in different ships, and they served together several times during their naval careers. They spent most time together when they were young captains in the West Indies in the 1780s. Collingwood's humane treatment of his crew and light punishment regime contrasted with Nelson's harsher methods.

However, when commander-in-chief, Collingwood was not popular with his captains, for he did not allow them to visit each other's ships, and his shyness resulted in very little entertaining and personal contact with his immediate subordinates.

in Aboukir Bay. He did not hesitate, though it was late in the day, and sailed straight into the unknown, shallow bay, allowing little time for the surprised French to prepare for battle. They were anyway handicapped by sickness and a shortage of food and water. Much of the action was fought in darkness, and the British superiority in seamanship and gunnery was overwhelming. Over 1st and 2nd August 1798 Nelson's ships gained the most decisive naval victory of the whole of the 18th century. 11 French ships of the line were captured or destroyed. The huge French flagship, *L'Orient* blew up; an estimated 5,000 Frenchmen died.

At home, with a government and country hungry for news, Lord Spencer at the Admiralty was being

---

Collingwood was second-in-command to Nelson at Trafalgar, and his ship, *Royal Sovereign*, which had just been docked, sailed faster than *Victory* into the Franco-Spanish fleet: it was probably the only time that Collingwood had outshone Nelson. He assumed command of the fleet after Nelson's death, writing home a dispatch of such power and feeling that George III could not believe that it had been penned by a naval officer.

His long and patient command of the Mediterranean, as Vice-Admiral Lord Collingwood, from 1805 until 1810, was relatively uneventful, but defensively it was very successful, minimising any advance by Napoleon's dominant land power.

Towards the end of his command, Collingwood was clearly very ill, but the Admiralty could not find an adequate successor to fill such an important command. Collingwood died on his way home in 1810, the Admiralty having at last agreed to relieve him of his command. He had spent only one year ashore in 17 years of war. ▪

criticised in the press through the late summer for sending such a young and inexperienced admiral to command such an important operation. The slow communications of the day resulted in rumours of success or failure buzzing around Europe. But on 26th September a naval officer arrived with Nelson's dispatches and certain news of Aboukir Bay finally reached London. Such a victory was celebrated joyfully throughout Britain, and it provided a great morale boost for the government. Lord Spencer, his political reputation safe, is supposed to have fainted with joy at hearing the news.

"BAND OF BROTHERS"

This quotation from Shakespeare's *Henry V* was used by Nelson to describe the captains of his squadron of 13 ships of the line which searched the eastern Mediterranean for Napoleon's Egyptian fleet and transports from early June 1798. They eventually found the French warships anchored in Aboukir Bay near Alexandria on 1st August, and the British destroyed all but two of them in the ensuing battle.

Nelson was fortunate to have been allotted very talented captains by the commander-in-chief of the Mediterranean, Admiral Lord St Vincent. For the most part they were young and aggressive, and their ships were well-manned, supplied with provisions and stores and in good order. The most distinguished were Thomas Troubridge, James Saumarez and the younger Samuel Hood. Nelson called them "the finest Squadron which ever graced the Ocean".

This powerful group, some of whom were older than Nelson, presented one particular problem. St Vincent had ordered that Troubridge, whom he favoured, should be appointed second-in-

Tactically, the British victory isolated Bonaparte and his army in the Levant. The victory brought Turkey, outraged by the French invasion of its dominions in Egypt, into the war against France and also encouraged the Russians in their hostility to France. The Kingdom of Naples was much encouraged in its resistance to the French. Britain was now dominant in the Mediterranean and her trade with the Levant was resumed. Anti-British hostilities in India, which had flared up with the news that the French had captured Egypt, were quieted.

command, whereas Saumarez was the senior, and moreover was less susceptible to Nelson's charm than the others.

Nelson managed this problem instinctively by not appointing a second-in-command, which in any case would have compromised his consultative style of command, and which today we might call a "flat structure", differing from the hierarchical outlook of almost all admirals of the time.

Nelson's flag captain Edward Berry described how Nelson would "have his captains on board the *Vanguard*, where he would fully develop to them his own ideas of the different and best modes of attack, and such plans as he proposed to execute when falling with the enemy... every one of the captains of his squadron was most thoroughly acquainted... by which signals became almost unnecessary".

This was undoubtedly an exaggeration, for Nelson issued several written sets of instructions, but it was a real innovation to be so open with his subordinates, and he continued this practice for the rest of his career. The critical point was made by Saumarez: "Unanimity," he entered in the journal he wrote for his wife, "I believe greater never existed in any squadron."* ∎

* Sugden, *Sword of Albion*, 79-82; Knight, *Pursuit of Victory*, 277-278

The Battle of the Nile enabled Britain to extend its reach into the south of Europe. Within two years Malta was finally captured from the French after a long siege; Britain then continued to hold it for 167 years. The battle dealt the French navy a psychological blow from which it never recovered. Thereafter French warships hesitated to venture out of port and the British navy tightened its blockade. While France remained dominant on the European Continent, control of the seas remained in British hands for the remainder of the Napoleonic Wars, a situation to be emphatically reinforced by the battle of Trafalgar seven years later.

What misjudgements did Nelson make at Naples during the summer of 1799?

After the victory at the Nile, Nelson arrived with his battered fleet at Naples on 22nd September 1798 to get his ships repaired, replenished and ready for sea again. Here he renewed his acquaintance with Sir William Hamilton, the British ambassador at the court of the Kingdom of the Two Sicilies (Naples and Sicily), and his wife Lady Emma Hamilton.

The King was weak and completely dominated by his wife, Maria Carolina. Partly because of her

*"The Destruction of 'L'Orient' at the Battle of the Nile, 1 August 1798",
by George Arnald.*

extrovert manners and through her singing and acting talents, Emma Hamilton was close to the Queen. Both had a penchant for intrigue, though it was the Queen who used their friendship to greatest advantage. These four characters were responsible for drawing Nelson into the extreme and bloodthirsty politics of Naples.

Maria Carolina was the sister of Marie Antoinette, who had been guillotined in Paris at the start of the French Revolution. As a result she was rabidly anti-republican, in stark contrast to many of the nobility and intellectuals who, influenced by the ideas of the enlightenment, were strongly republican. It was very much a divided country, marked by violence between royalist and republican mobs. Nelson supported the royalists to a point which was to run against British interests.

Within three months he was encouraging the Neapolitan court with their under-resourced army to invade Rome. By the late winter of 1798 the army had retreated in confusion, and the military situation became so disastrous that late at night on Christmas Eve, he evacuated the royal family and the Hamiltons in his flagship to Palermo. For the first half of 1799, his ships were based at Palermo, where, as a rear-admiral with virtually no staff, Nelson had very wide responsibilities, including the command of all British ships in the eastern Mediterranean. He felt neglected by the British government, and had little communication with London. He soon became dependent upon Emma for emotional support and by the summer of 1799 the relationship had gone beyond dalliance. Exhausted by his duties and besotted with Emma, he began to make mistakes.

In June the Naples government asked him to bring the British fleet back to Naples, which by then had already seen much bloodshed. The French had occupied the kingdom for six months, but their army had been withdrawn northwards to fight elsewhere, leaving a small force to man the two fortresses that dominated the city. In mid-June a royalist mob from Calabria had set upon the republicans with much slaughter. The remnants of the republican forces withdrew into two fortresses, ejecting the French. A surrender agreement was drawn up between the royalists and republicans. It was witnessed by a junior British naval captain, Edward Foote, who commanded the *Seahorse,* stationed on blockade duty in Naples Bay.

At this point, 25th June, Nelson and the Hamiltons (but, crucially, not the King and Queen) arrived in Naples Bay with the British fleet of 18 ships of the line. One of Nelson's first acts was to put Thomas Troubridge ashore with 500 marines and seamen to try to keep order. It is difficult to understand exactly the events of the next few days, but undoubtedly Nelson repudiated the republicans' surrender agreement with the royalists. The republicans were taken prisoner by the British and put in local vessels anchored in the Bay.

Nelson was already intervening far too much in local politics, and the good name of the British government suffered at a very difficult time in the war. But his next misjudgement was to bring him further and lasting criticism. One of the Neapolitan admirals, Caracciolo, had deserted to the republicans and had been captured. Nelson was persuaded to allow an immediate court martial by Neapolitan naval officers, which returned a verdict of guilty, the admiral to be hanged within two hours. It would have been wise to have delayed this execution until the king arrived to confirm the decision, but not only did Nelson allow it go ahead immediately, but he also rejected Caracciolo's plea to be shot, according to the dictates of his rank. Nelson was undoubtedly encouraged to have no mercy by Emma Hamilton, the mouthpiece of the anti-republican queen.

Two days later Nelson brought the Neapolitan vessels carrying the republican prisoners under the guns of British ships, and took some of them on board. At this point several of his captains protested at this interference in the internal affairs of Naples, but Nelson rejected these protests outright. "I will be obeyed," he said: his consensual style of command had deserted him. The trials of the republicans continued for the next 40 days, during which time Nelson kept the British fleet in Naples Bay to ensure that the royalists could consolidate their position.

EMMA HAMILTON

Emma Lyon was born in Neston on The Wirral peninsula in Cheshire, the daughter of a blacksmith. She went to London as a housemaid and became a kept woman and one of the beauties of the age. Her first "protector" was Sir Harry Featherstonhaugh, followed by MP Charles Greville, who passed her on to his maternal uncle, Sir William Hamilton, widower and British Minister at Naples. In March 1785 Emma went to Naples where she became Hamilton's mistress and then, in September 1791, his wife. Hamilton was 60, 34 years older than Emma. Her extrovert personality, and her talent for languages and for singing, made her a great favourite at the Neapolitan court.

In 1793 the Hamiltons met Nelson briefly when he called into Naples. On his return to Naples in September 1798 after his triumph at the Nile

In order to remain in Naples, Nelson committed a cardinal British naval sin. In July he flatly disobeyed a direct order from his senior officer, Admiral Lord Keith, who conveyed the Admiralty's order to Nelson to bring his ships to join Keith at Minorca to combine the whole British Mediterranean fleet. The island, captured the previous year from the Spaniards, was under threat. Nelson refused to leave Naples, arguing that it was more important than anything else in the Mediterranean. No harm did come to Minorca, but no other admiral would have got away with such flagrant disobedience of important orders.

The involvement in drawn-out bloodshed in

he stayed with them. Emma became emotionally involved with Nelson in 1799 and his mistress soon afterwards. The trio left Italy in 1800 and travelled across Europe, home to England, with Emma pregnant.

The child, Horatia, was born at the end of January 1801, at the same time as Nelson separated from his wife, Fanny. A second child, who was short-lived, may have been born in 1803 or 1804.

When Nelson came ashore from his command of the Channel squadron in October 1801, he returned to Merton Place, south of London, which Emma had found. She furnished and managed it for him, though William Hamilton kept a house in Piccadilly which was officially her home.

After Nelson's death, she took to drink, and, unable to manage money, died in debt in Calais. The *Morning Post* obituary: "in private life she was a humane and generous woman, intoxicated with the flattery and admiration which attended her in a rank of life so different from the obscure condition of her early days".*■
* Fraser, *Beloved Emma*, 372-373

Naples damaged the British cause in Europe. By a modern estimate, 8,000 republicans were tried, more than a thousand exiled and several thousand put into prison. It was, however, the 120 executions in Naples that made the headlines. Some prisoners were beheaded, others were hanged in the city – where the story lives on – with the street urchins or *tirapiedi* swinging on the feet of the victims. The question still asked today is: were the republicans tricked into surrendering?

Nelson was still instinctively a frigate captain, accustomed to swift tactical decisions. He had no patience with long deliberations, or wider considerations of the political implications of decisions of life and death. At this point the 40-year-old naval officer was out of his depth, taking advice only from Emma Hamilton. Sir William Hamilton, the ambassador who should have given him dispassionate guidance, had been in Naples for nearly 30 years, had "gone native" and was too close to the queen for independent judgement. One week in June 1799 in a career of 35 years besmirched Nelson's reputation forever.

Did Nelson trick the Danes at Copenhagen in 1801?

Through the 1790s Russia's enmity towards French Revolutionary ideology had resulted in good relations with Britain. The lesser Baltic States of Sweden, Prussia and Denmark had followed suit. The Baltic was the source of the strategic war materials of the age, important to both Britain and France, for it supplied the very large quantities of timber, pitch and hemp that were needed to build the merchant ships and warships of Europe. However, Britain's efforts to prevent these products being shipped to France, by insisting on its right of search of neutral vessels, united the Baltic States against Britain, and after the succession of the anglophobe Tsar Paul I in Russia in 1796, relations began to deteriorate. In 1800 Danish warships resisted British warships who tried to search a Danish convoy and on 16th December 1800 the Baltic States signed the Northern Convention to form an "armed neutrality" against Britain. Despite this, there remained a strong link between the two countries, for the Danish crown prince was a nephew of King George III of England.

The most vulnerable of the signatories was Denmark as it controlled the entry to the Baltic through the Sound, where Copenhagen was situated. Concerned that entry to the Baltic might be blocked, in December 1800 the British government began planning to send a powerful naval fleet to the Sound to force Denmark to renounce the Convention, and then to proceed up the Baltic to attack the Russian fleet. Admiral Sir Hyde Parker was to command the fleet, with Nelson as his second in command. The fleet gathered in the

Yarmouth Roads (off the Norfolk coast) with Nelson's flag in the *St George* (90). It sailed for the Baltic in stormy weather on 13th March 1801. In Copenhagen Danish and British diplomats were still talking, but were getting nowhere.

Relations between Hyde Parker and Nelson were frosty, though they improved as the fleet approached the Danish coast. By 23rd March all diplomatic negotiations in Copenhagen had broken down, but Hyde Parker, who had a reputation for dithering, still hoped to avoid the hostile Danes by sailing the fleet through the Great Belt. No one was confident that the deep-draught warships could get through, so Parker then changed his mind and headed for the Sound again. Nelson fulminated, wanting to attack the Danes immediately, and indeed this delay enabled them, now thoroughly alarmed, to make battle preparations. A line of assorted Danish warships was moored north and south, off Copenhagen on the western side of the Hollander Deep.

It was agreed that Nelson should command an advance squadron of seven 74-gun and four 64-gun ships, while Parker stayed offshore with the deeper-draught larger warships. Nelson transferred his flag to the *Elephant* (74). On 1st April his ships sailed south and anchored off the Middle Ground, the shoal off Copenhagen. During the night the British surveyed the shallow waters of the Hollander Deep, for the Danes had removed all navigational marks. Nelson and his captains had dinner together and Nelson laid out his plans to them. During the night the wind went to the south, the direction that Nelson needed to sail round the Middle Ground and to the north towards the Danish line.

At 10.15 on the morning of 2nd April he gave the order to weigh anchor and the British warships sailed around the south of the Middle Ground and towards Copenhagen, though one immediately grounded on the shoal. Slowly the ships moved northwards to oppose the Danish line and anchored, as at the Nile, by the stern, though rather further away than Nelson had wanted. By 11.45 all the British ships were engaged. In the southern part of the line, the British had outgunned the Danes by 496 guns to 244; in the middle section the margin was 352 to 202; only in the northern sector did the number of guns favour the Danes. In spite of being heavily outgunned, Danish resistance was stubborn and heroic, and they took heavy casualties before, one by one, they retired from the conflict.

At about one o'clock, Admiral Parker, anxiously observing the bombardment and heavy smoke from five miles away, hoisted his famous signal to "Discontinue the Action". He claimed that it was to give Nelson the option of withdrawing to save his reputation. Nelson, of course, ignored the signal and the *Elephant* retained the signal for "Close Action". It was at this point that Nelson was supposed to have put his telescope to his blind eye, saying "I really do not see the signal". It is a good story, though unverified. Throughout the battle, Nelson was accompanied on deck by an army officer, Lieutenant-Colonel William Stewart, who wrote a detailed narrative of the battle a few days after it, in which there was no suggestion of the supposed incident. However, we cannot be sure.[*]

In spite of their dominance and strength, not all was going well for the British. Several ships were grounded, though all continued firing. More Danish ships stopped firing, their damage and casualties too heavy for them to continue. It was at this point that Nelson sent a message on shore to the Danish

[*] Sugden, *Sword of Albion*, 442-444

THE FIRST BIOGRAPHIES OF NELSON

The first biography of Nelson appeared around 1801 and there has been a steady stream of them since his death, in addition to well over 1,500 books on the broader subject of Nelson and the wars against France. Robert Southey's *Life of Nelson*, published in 1813, written very accessibly and going through a plethora of editions, has never been out of print. Famously,

Southey criticised Nelson's conduct at Naples. For instance, the decision to hang the Italian admiral Caracciolo deserved "a severe and unqualified condemnation".[*]

Perhaps the most interesting, viewed from today, was the biography written at the end of the 19th century by the influential American admiral, Alfred Thayer Mahan. His 1899 *Life of Nelson* expanded on his long historical campaign – which began with his *Influence of Sea Power on History* (1893) – to persuade politicians in Washington of the need for America to build up its fleet. (By all accounts, his

Crown Prince, addressed "To his Brothers, the Danes", in which he proposed a truce. Nelson was not really in sufficiently a dominant position to demand a truce. He maintained that his motive for sending the message was humanitarian – to stop useless slaughter. Nevertheless, a number of senior officers were in no doubt that Nelson's motives were more in the nature of a trick, a cover for weakness. Colonel Stewart reported back home, "for victorious as we were, the narrowness of the Channel in which our ships were engaged & the commanding batteries on shore had left our Ships, six of which were aground, in a most perilous

principal success was to persuade the Kaiser to expand the German fleet!)

Mahan became embroiled in a scholarly controversy at the time of the centenary of Trafalgar in 1905. He backed up the British historian Sir John Knox Laughton in a bitter dispute in the press and scholarly journals which took place between 1897 and 1908. Their opponent was F.P. Badham, a descendant of Captain Edward Foote, who had made the agreement with the republicans in Naples which Nelson repudiated. Badham condemned Nelson utterly, while the establishment historians attempted to refute his arguments. Laughton, too, had contemporary reasons, with the beginning of a European armaments race, to keep Nelson's reputation beyond reproach. An interesting attempt to find historical proof one way or the other was the dispassionate judgement displayed by the scholar H.C. Gutteridge in *Nelson and the Neapolitan Jacobins* (1903). We shall never know quite what happened in the summer of 1799 in Naples, but it is a stain on Nelson's reputation which has remained to this day. ∎

* Southey, *Life of Nelson*, 201

situation..."[*]

Whatever the motive, the British strategy to keep the Baltic open was upheld, a position which was bolstered by the news of the assassination of Tsar Paul I, received soon after the battle. Nelson conducted the truce negotiations, re-establishing his reputation after his fall from grace because of his involvement with Emma Hamilton. Hyde Parker was recalled, and Nelson was made commander-in-chief of the Baltic and a viscount. He took risk after risk at Copenhagen, but won through.

How successful was Nelson's command of the anti-invasion forces in the Channel?

On 1st July 1801 Nelson arrived back in England after his successful campaign in the Baltic. Within three weeks he was ordered to sea again. His instructions from the Board of Admiralty ran: "we have appointed your Lordship Commander-in-Chief of a squadron of His Majesty's ships... to be employed on a particular service... in the defence of the mouths of the Thames and Medway,

[*] National Maritime Museum, AGC/14/27, 6 April 1801

and all that part of the coasts of Sussex, Kent and Essex, comprised between Beachy Head and Orfordness". Once he was satisfied with defensive measures, Nelson was to find a means "for blocking up or destroying if practicable, the enemy's vessels and craft in the ports wherein they may be assembled..."*

Invasion had always been an integral part of French war strategy and the threat to Britain was ever present: a large and growing army was stationed ready in the French Channel ports. With their success at sea, it might seem that the British were in a strong position. In addition to the string of naval victories in which Nelson had played a part, the Dutch navy had been overwhelmed at Camperdown in 1797 and at Den Helder in 1799. After a successful landing at Aboukir Bay in 1801, an expeditionary force under Sir Ralph Abercromby had defeated the French army in Egypt.

However, France was still dominant on the Continent and Britain at this time was diplomatically isolated. Austria had sued for peace. Bonaparte had abandoned his army in the Levant in August 1799 and, dodging the British navy, had slipped back into France on a small merchant ship. He was now consolidating his power in Paris as First Consul. Political change had come to London too. On 19th February 1801 William Pitt had resigned after 17 years as prime minister. Henry

* Morrison, II, 1578, 26 July 1801

Addington took over the government. Nelson's relations with him were always more friendly than with the austere Pitt.

At the same time, war fatigue had taken hold in Britain and elsewhere in Europe. People wanted peace. Addington's government decided to open peace negotiations with France. This did not, however, necessarily mean that Napoleon would slacken his war effort. Nelson and many other naval officers thought the French invasion threat was merely bluff. Opposition newspapers also held this view. But it had to be taken seriously and there is no doubt that the French armies at the Channel ports applied pressure on the British government while peace talks proceeded. It was against this background that Nelson assumed command of his fleet of shallow-drafted small vessels, suitable for the coastal waters around the south-east of England. He first had 70 under his orders; by September this had increased to 148.

He moved rapidly by coach through Kent, stopping at Sheerness and Faversham, organising and coordinating the maritime defence forces. Manpower, as ever, was short. He stirred up the Sea Fencibles, a naval militia notoriously reluctant to come forward in spite of the fact that they received the king's shilling. He received much applause and adulation from the population after his recent feats: this was exactly what Addington wanted him for, to whip up support for the vigorous defence of the country.

Nelson hoisted his flag in the *Medusa*, a new 38-gun frigate, gathered his bomb vessels and on 4th and 5th August they bombarded Boulogne. The target was the fleet of invasion barges. Little damage was done to them, however, although psychologically it might have been effective. He withdrew, and sailed in the *Medusa* up to Harwich, the northernmost point of his command, to inspect ships and defences. On 10th August Lord St Vincent, now First Lord of the Admiralty, wrote to Nelson informing him of intelligence reports from Paris: Bonaparte was still threatening invasion. Another effort was needed.

Nelson returned to Boulogne again, but after the relative failure of the bombardment, turned to the idea of a surprise night attack, as he had done at Tenerife, but this was also unsuccessful. On 16th August, a moonless night, the launches lost touch with each other, and when they attacked the French defence vessels, the boarders found that they were protected with nets and chains. All the British attacks were repelled and casualties were heavy.

As the early autumn passed, Nelson remained on board a frigate, anchored in the Downs, miserable at being apart from Emma. He was also much saddened by the severe wound that had been inflicted on one his young captains, Edward Thornborough Parker, who had led a boarding party and who was soon to die from his injuries. For a period Emma was on shore at Deal with Sir William, and there were visits ashore, and other members of his family came to see him. Though this cheered him, there was not much else to be thankful for. Nelson was often seasick in rough weather, a malady to which he was always prone in small ships. He protested repeatedly to the Board of Admiralty that he was being kept unnecessarily in his command. In reality, he was a naturally aggressive admiral who fretted in this defensive role.

On 1st October peace preliminaries with France were signed in London. Prime Minister Addington wrote to Nelson ten days later: "it is of the utmost importance to the Interests of your Country that

MODERN BIOGRAPHIES OF NELSON

Carola Oman's *Nelson* (1947) was a *tour de force*, since she was the first author able to use the collection of letters bought by John Wilson Croker, Secretary to the Admiralty, in 1817. This consists of more than 2,000 letters received by Nelson. Croker had purchased them with government money to keep any scandal away from public view, though some of them were made available to Sir Harris Nicolas. Later in the 19th century they had been acquired by Sir Thomas Phillipps, the great Victorian collector. Only when they were purchased for the National Maritime Museum in 1946 by Sir James Caird were they free to be used in total, 140 years after Nelson's death. Oman brought new material and a fresh eye to the story.

Other biographies of Nelson were published in the second half of the 20th century, most notably by Tom Pocock, but the bicentenary of the battle of Trafalgar in 2005 saw a deluge of some 40 titles about Nelson, his subordinates and aspects of the battle. The your flag should be flying until the Definitive treaty is signed. You will have seen the ship safe into Port and may close with honour a career of unexampled success & glory".[*] But the Prime Minister did not get his way. After Nelson protested, the Admiralty relented and he received permission to strike his flag and go on shore. (In contrast, and to show how much the government went out of its way to please Nelson, his friend, William Cornwallis, commanding the fleet off Brest, was not allowed ashore for another six months.)

[*] Knight, *Pursuit of Victory*, 417

---

division of the historians over the events in Naples was not so public as in 1905, but the two sides are as far away as ever. Terry Coleman characterised Nelson as a "natural-born predator, pitiless and a good hater", and at Naples, "duplicitous and politically inept".[*] Andrew Lambert, on the other hand, pours scorn on the "Black Legend" of Naples and claims that "Nelson handled the events of that summer with his customary skill". On the question of the breaking of the armistice and the death of Caracciolo, Lambert cannot believe that "such unmitigated nonsense should have persisted in the public consciousness", while "Southey's accusation of dishonourable public conduct" is "entirely without foundation".[**]

Of the bicentenary biographies, John Sugden's even-handed two-volume *A Dream of Glory* (2004) and *The Sword of Albion* (2012) stands out. This author's *Pursuit of Victory* (2005) was put on the United States Navy's prescribed senior officers' professional reading list, and had the unusual distinction of being translated into French in 2015. ∎

[*] Coleman, *Nelson*, 81-21
[**] Lambert, *Britannia's God of War*, 365, 369, 372

Had Nelson made a difference? It was perhaps a misjudgement to take the risks he took in the second attack on Boulogne, but Nelson was under pressure from politicians to make a show of British resolve. He was essentially fulfilling a political role by bringing pressure to match that being exercised by Napoleon. Addington was pleased enough. It was not until 25th March 1802 that the Definitive Treaty of Peace with France was signed at Amiens. It signed away much of British overseas territorial gains, but few felt confident of a lasting peace. Britain's population and finances, however, at least gained some respite.

What was Nelson's state of mind at Merton during the Peace of Amiens?

During the short Peace of Amiens between March 1802 and May 1803, Nelson had a settled existence for the first time since the war began in 1793. While he was still at sea, Emma Hamilton had found Merton Place, a moderately large house with a small estate, seven miles south of London, near Wimbledon. With her enthusiastic support, he purchased it, sight unseen, signing the documents in October 1801 when he came ashore from his command of the anti-invasion flotilla. There is little doubt that Nelson loved Merton, and took a great interest in the details of running the farm and the grounds, and his feelings for Emma were passionate. This has led commentators to christen this period of his life as "Paradise" Merton. It was, however, a bitter-sweet time, and there were many tensions and worries, domestic, social and financial.

The first problem was the hostile view of the outside world of Nelson's abandonment of his wife Fanny for Emma. It was, of course, out of the question for Nelson and Emma to be seen in polite society. Though there were many visitors, and local friends were made, many of Nelson's naval colleagues failed to call at Merton. He spent time in London, and spoke in the House of Lords, but he continued to feel that he was not accepted by the establishment. He exchanged a spirited and bad-tempered correspondence with the First Lord of the Admiralty, Lord St Vincent, over the failure of the government to issue medals to those who distinguished themselves at the battle of Copenhagen.

Some remained loyal. Lord Minto, formerly Sir Gilbert Elliot, a friend since the Corsica days at the beginning of the war, visited, though not with his wife, to whom he reported critically on Emma:

> She goes on cramming Nelson with trowelfuls of
> flattery, which he goes on taking as quietly as a
> child does pap... the whole house, staircase and
> all, are covered with nothing but pictures of her
> and him... an excess of vanity which counteracts

its own purpose. If it was Lady H's house there might be a pretence for it; to make his own a mere looking-glass to view himself all day is bad taste.[*]

Tensions were also present within Merton, for Emma still feared that Nelson would be reconciled with Fanny, and she sent vituperative letters on the subject (she called Fanny "Tom Tit") to other members of the family. All this was accentuated by occasional visits of Horatia, Nelson's child by Emma, who lived nearby, but could only be seen discreetly by close family. William Hamilton's own standing weakened too, for his grand family disowned him. The older man's tolerance of the three-sided relationship seems at this distance to

[*]   Minto, III, 241-243, 22 March 1802

THE BRONTE ESTATE IN SICILY

King Ferdinand of Naples created Nelson the Duke of Bronte for saving the Kingdom of Naples in July 1799. The King purchased the rights of the 40,000-acre Bronte Estate on the slopes of Mount Etna in Sicily from the Grande Hospital at Palermo, and raised it to the status of a Duchy. George III gave permission for Nelson to use the title and thereafter he signed himself "Nelson and Bronte".

Nelson wished to develop the estate. He installed John Graefer, a talented manager, who set about building a farmhouse, but his attempts to introduce new farming methods were lost on Sicilian agricultural workers, who were wedded to old ways. Few of the intended developments took be extraordinarily patient, but he had a great deal to lose, and as time went on he was more and more in London, pursuing his interests at the British Museum and the Society of Antiquaries.

There were two close family deaths. Nelson had been in the Baltic when he had heard about his favourite brother, Maurice, who had died in March 1801 only a month after he had gained his long-sought after promotion in the Navy Office. Nelson's father, Edmund, followed in April 1802. Edmund had become reconciled to Nelson, though probably not to Emma, and had stayed at Merton, but his sympathies were still with Fanny. Nelson did not attend his father's funeral in Norfolk, pleading ill health: probably he could not face the gossip of Burnham Thorpe, which he had not visited since he

---

place as Graefer died in 1802, but as a result of help from Abraham Gibbs, a banker in Palermo, the estate did continue to yield a modest income. *

Nelson had plans to retire to Bronte with Emma Hamilton. When, for instance, he came back from Europe in 1801, he called to see the Neapolitan minister in London to see if this might be possible in peacetime.** But Nelson never saw it again, as later that year he purchased Merton near Wimbledon, and put his emotions and capital into his life there. The estate passed down through Nelson's niece Charlotte, who married into the Bridport family, which owned it until it was sold in the 1980s to the Commune of Bronte. Some of the family's naval paintings and artefacts still remain there. ∎

* Jane Knight, 'Bronte Estate',138-141
** Sugden, *Sword of Albion*, 402-403, 489

had left for the war, and was never to see again.

The other problem was a constant shortage of money. Nelson had many calls on his generosity, particularly from his family, who equated his fame with riches, and he found it difficult to resist such requests. Money needed to be spent on the house, while Emma's extravagant tendencies in both purchases and entertaining had to be met. He also bought a considerable amount of land, the main purchase being in 1803 from a local farmer. His Merton estate expanded from the one and a quarter acres originally purchased until, by 1803, it measured 114 acres.[*]

At the same time, he was corresponding with John Graefer, his manager at Bronte, and sending out modern farming equipment and seed to Sicily. This yielded nothing: Graefer died, and Nelson was never to see the estate he had hoped one day to live on in peaceful times. He never had enough capital to live in the style to which he thought he was entitled, and which he thought that the world would expect of Britain's most famous admiral.

To get away from these cares, Nelson, William and Emma Hamilton set off in late July 1802 for a six-week holiday to Milford in South Wales. William had inherited land in Pembrokeshire from his first wife, and his nephew Charles Greville was attempting to develop the town, especially by establishing a local shipbuilding industry, with an

[*] Sugden, *Sword of Albion*, 541

eye to supplying warships for the navy. The purpose of the journey was, therefore, to bring publicity to the venture by associating Nelson's name with it. The journey, which included stops at Oxford, Ludlow and Monmouth, became a triumphal progress, with honours and ceremonies at every stop. It was a happy time.

But it was not to last. At the end of the winter, in April 1803, William Hamilton died in Emma's arms and with Nelson holding his hand. Emma's grief was prolonged and very public, as well it might be, for her financial future was now uncertain, and without Hamilton there could be no pretence if Nelson and Emma were to spend time together. Besides, she was pregnant with a second child. Yet all this domestic upheaval was soon cast into the background. British government relations with Napoleonic France were fast deteriorating and war was declared in May 1803. Nelson was appointed commander-in-chief in the Mediterranean and was soon back at sea, amongst the certainties of rank and of relationships, secure on his quarter-deck. Emma's child did not survive.

TEN FACTS ABOUT
HMS *VICTORY*

1.

Victory measured 2,162 tons, was 186 feet along the gun deck and had a beam of nearly 52 feet. Her maximum draft when fully loaded was 25ft.

2.

She had 100 guns. At the time of Trafalgar there were thirty 32-pounders on the lower gun deck, twenty-eight 24-pounders on the middle gun deck, thirty 12-pounders on the upper gun deck and ten 6-pounders on the quarter deck. There were also two 68lb carronades on the forecastle, devastating at short range.

3.

Victory was designed by Sir Thomas Slade, the most celebrated 18th-century Surveyor of the Navy, and her keel was laid at Chatham dockyard in 1759. Launched in 1765, she was forty years old when she fought at Trafalgar.

4.

She was thus very old in an age when the active service of warships built of oak averaged only 12 years, but she sailed so well and steadily and was so popular with admirals that she was repaired and refitted many times. In 1799, worn out after continuous service during the French Revolutionary War, she was laid up and ordered to be converted into a hospital ship.

5.

She was, however, reprieved and was docked at Chatham in 1800 for a repair, but when docked was found to be in a far worse state than anticipated. The final repair bill when she was undocked in April 1803 was £70,000, an enormous sum; but she was in good condition for the next few vital years.

6.

Her muster book demonstrates that in 1805 she had 875 crew. She also had 47 "supernumeraries" which accounted for Nelson and his staff. She had the capacity to stow 380 tons of water in barrels and 300 tons of provisions, which would last six months, though this would be supplemented by fresh foodstuffs whenever possible.

7.

At Trafalgar the *Victory* fired 3,041 shots in four hours and 20 minutes of firing: the 32-pounders fired 997, the 24-pounders 872 and the 12-pounders 800. This was an average of seven shots an hour per gun. Seven and a half tons of gunpowder were expended, three tons of "junk" for wadding, 3,000 musket balls and 2,000 pistol balls.

8.

At Trafalgar 54 men were killed, 25 dangerously wounded, 12 badly wounded and 42 slightly wounded. Virtually all these casualties were from the quarter-deck, poop and forecastle.

9.

After Trafalgar the *Victory* served in the Baltic until 1812 when she was laid up and saw no further active service. During her active service from 1778 to 1812 the *Victory* served as the flagship for 17 admirals.

10.

She remained at anchor in Portsmouth harbour until 1922 after which she was found to be sinking, when she was docked in order to save her. From 1932 until the present she has served as flagship in dock for senior shore-based admirals and the endless task of maintaining her continues.

HMS Victory in The Battle of Trafalgar *by J. M. W. Turner (1775-1851)*

How did Nelson cope as commander-in-chief in the Mediterranean?

Nelson's fame rests principally on skilful decisions quickly taken at the height of the great battles of the Revolutionary War. However, his reputation for leadership and management should also take account of very long periods at sea when almost no guns were fired in anger. The most important time was his 15-month period as commander-in-chief, Mediterranean, from the outbreak of the Napoleonic war after the Peace of Amiens in May 1803 to the pursuit of the French fleet over the Atlantic in the summer of 1805.

The first of his difficulties was maintaining communications with England, and there were long periods in which he received no letters or dispatches. He had also to collect and assess local intelligence. One of the bigger problems was to anticipate Spanish intentions, for she was likely to throw in her lot with France. In the event she declared war on Britain in December 1804, as a result of British warships capturing silver ships from Spanish South America off Cadiz – a bungled operation carried out without Nelson's knowledge. As well as this, he not only had to defend Malta, captured in 1800 from the French, but also to ensure that it was fed, for the island could not sustain itself. This depended on defending Sicily, where much wheat was grown, and also upon maintaining good relations with the North African states, keeping in touch with British consuls there, to make sure that supplies of grain and cattle reached the island, both for its inhabitants and for resupplying British ships. There was also the eastern Mediterranean, relations with the Balkans, the Turks and Russia to worry about.

But above all his task was to watch the growing French fleet in Toulon, to ensure that it did not break out and strike at one of the British weak points, attempting an invasion of Ireland, for example, or having another go at Egypt. It might be thought that this was easy, but for long periods the margin between the number of Nelson's ships and those of the French was very slim. To blockade Toulon was very difficult as there were no nearby friendly ports to provide shelter for repairs and maintenance of his ships or to replenish his stores. North-westerly winds, often gales in winter, blew his fleet away from the French coast. He used the system of "open" rather than "close" blockade, keeping his fleet well away from the shore, below the horizon, so that the French might be tempted to send their fleet out which would enable him to bring it to action.

Supporting this blockade with food and stores was a constant problem, and he had to cope with a constant majority of his ships in need of repair and maintenance. Nelson reckoned that Malta was too far away and downwind to support his fleet off Toulon, so that his ships used two anchorages in Sardinia: the best was Agincourt Sound in the north of the island, a sheltered harbour in which storeships and victualling transports transferred their cargoes to the warships, while Pula in the south was useful because sweet drinking water was available all the year round even in the hot summer months.

Nelson never had less than 7,000 men to feed and sustain, and to do that he needed a constant supply of wood for fuel and water. Yet his men were healthy, with plentiful supplies of lemons to combat

NELSON'S LETTERS

By the time he had reached flag rank, Nelson was writing hundreds of letters a year. He wrote fluent and lively prose, though rarely mentioned what he was feeling. When at sea as commander-in-chief, he signed many more orders and dispatches, most of which are in the Admiralty papers in the National Archives at Kew. Sadly, he destroyed most of Emma Hamilton's letters to him.

The most important personal manuscript collections are the 129 volumes of Nelson and Hamilton correspondence in the British Library, and several collections of correspondence in the National Maritime Museum, Greenwich. Long letters of particular interest in Nelson's immediately recognisable left hand script fetch high prices at auction, far higher than museums and archives can now afford, and thus many are in the hands of private collectors.

Contemporary and Victorian susceptibilities over Nelson's affair with Emma Hamilton initially blighted publication of his corres-pondence. The first major collection of letters was published by James Stanier scurvy and a good victualling system, including Spanish dollars to buy fresh food. However, discipline became more of a problem when French trade in the Mediterranean dried up, such was the dominance of Britain at sea, because prize money could no longer be used as an incentive for the crews. Nevertheless, time at these anchorages was kept to a minimum and Nelson kept his fleet at sea for very long periods all year round.

His final set of tasks was to keep British trade moving, and particularly to get the Levant trade, primarily dried fruit, spices, olive oil and wine,

---

Clarke and John M'Arthur in 1809, but the deletions (and additions) that they inflicted on the manuscripts, which Colin White called "editorial vandalism", make these two large volumes completely untrustworthy. His relations with Emma Hamilton were not even mentioned, although in 1814 the anonymously published *Letters of Lord Nelson to Lady Hamilton* left little doubt as to the nature of the relationship.

No further edition of Nelson letters was attempted until 1846 when Sir Nicholas Harris Nicolas produced the admirable seven-volume *Dispatches and Letters*, though this great work is by nowhere near complete. It was closely

followed by the two volumes of Thomas Pettigrew in 1849, which included more letters involving Lady Hamilton. Many gaps were filled by the collector, Alfred Morrison, when he published privately transcripts of the letters in his possession in 1893, though sets of this two-volume work are rare as only 600 copies were printed.

Some smaller collections of documents have been published during the 20th century, but no comprehensive attempt to complete all known letters was made until Colin White's *Nelson: the New Letters*, but even he did not capture them all. In all, 6,500 letters are in print. ∎

home to England from Greek and Turkish ports. This was done by gathering the merchant ships at Malta, which then formed into large convoys, escorted by some of Nelson's smaller warships. Nelson never stopped complaining about the meagre number of smaller warships available to him. He also needed them for escorting merchant ships with cargoes of timber and hemp from the Black Sea, and to do the same for convoys from North Africa. French and North African privateers were ever a threat.

Naturally anxious, he drove himself hard during this period and his health suffered. He hinted to the Admiralty that this was a problem, but never actually asked to be relieved. His consistent performance, in contrast to his previous erratic time in the Mediterranean, was a remarkable achievement.

Why did he have to chase the French fleet across the Atlantic?

Napoleon's plan in 1805 was to decoy the British fleet to the West Indies so that the Channel would be denuded of British ships for a short time, to enable his invasion barges to cross the Channel. If the French and Spanish fleet was able to capture a British West Indian island as part of the operation, so much the better.

The French fleet under Admiral Pierre Ville-neuve broke out of Toulon on 17th January 1805 and it was to elude Nelson for nine months. Manned by inexperienced crews unused to time at sea, bad weather eventually caused enough damage to compel Villeneuve to return to Toulon. Nelson first received the news of the French break-out on 19th January when anchored, taking on provisions and water in the north of Sardinia. He believed that the French were heading eastwards towards Egypt and he sailed there to ensure that the eastern Mediter-ranean was safe. When the French again emerged from Toulon, he missed them. It was not until early May that he headed towards the Straits of Gibraltar. On 10th May, anchored in Lagos Bay, Portugal, he learnt that the French, now joined by the Spanish under the command of Admiral Gravina, had sailed to the West Indies a month earlier.

With great luck, Nelson met with a convoy of victualling transports from England which enabled him to store his ships quickly and he sailed his fleet of ten ships of the line and three frigates as fast as he could across the Atlantic. From 20th May to 3rd June the fleet sailed 2,130 miles, averaging 142 miles a day, the highest run being 190 miles, gaining ten days on the French, arriving at Carlisle Bay, Barbados on 4th June.

He then again missed the enemy in the West Indies, acting on faulty intelligence which misled him into thinking that the French had turned south to attack Trinidad. In fact they had turned north, but soon heard about Nelson's pursuit of them. With sickly crews, Villeneuve and Gravina immediately headed back to Europe, having achieved virtually nothing. No West Indian island had been lost to the French. Villeneuve headed for Ferrol in Northern Spain.

Nothing illustrated Nelson's determination to bring the enemy to battle more than his decision to pursue them at all costs. On 14th June he headed back to Europe without taking on more water or fresh provisions. Winds were light. Progress was slow. On board the *Victory* it was found that some of the casks of fresh water in the hold had leaked. The crew were rationed, discipline relaxed, drunkenness, quarrelling and fighting increased: on one day on board the *Victory*, 22nd June, 14 men were given a total of 432 lashes. Then Nelson's luck turned. On a calm day he met an American merchant ship and purchased 40 head of cattle, fresh meat for the fleet. A fortnight later, on a windless day in the mid-Atlantic, 20 tons of water were transferred from another ship.

It had been a remarkable effort. On 17th July 1805, as he approached Gibraltar, Nelson entered in his private journal, "3,227 miles out, 3,459 back, average per day, thirty-four leagues, wanting nine miles". Two days later, anchored in Rosia Bay, Gibraltar, he wrote: "I went on shore for the first time since the 16th of June 1803; and from having my foot out of the *Victory*, two years, wanting ten days".[*]

The crossing and re-crossing of the Atlantic showed Nelson as a consummate risk-taker, but he did it with a sophisticated, professional assessment of the odds. He was very methodical. For instance, he kept a personal daily weather log. Cuthbert Collingwood was to write to a naval friend soon after Nelson's death: "Everything seemed, as if by enchantment, to prosper under his direction. But it was the effect of system, and nice combination, not of chance."[**]

This pursuit of the French and Spanish had its psychological effect. Villeneuve, against Napoleon's orders, sailed south to find safe haven in Cadiz harbour. Two months later, Nelson was to find them not far from their safe harbour, off Cape Trafalgar.

What did the British victory at Trafalgar achieve?

After 25 days in Merton and London, Nelson set sail from Spithead in the *Victory*, which had been rapidly refurbished and stored. On 28th September 1805 he relieved Collingwood of the command of the fleet which was blockading the French and Spanish fleets inside Cadiz harbour. Nelson did not

[*]   British Library, Private Journal, Add. Mss 34968
[**]   Knight, *Pursuit of Victory*, 556

know more than a dozen of the captains, but by dinners and discussions he ensured they knew his mind and the tactics he would use if it came to battle. As at Toulon, he kept his fleet well out to sea, below the horizon and out of sight, with Cadiz watched by a single frigate which could transmit flag signals.

On 18th October the combined French and Spanish fleet left Cadiz. Hounded by Napoleon, who wanted action, the French admiral Pierre Villeneuve was provoked into sailing, though he had no clear objective. Two days later, thinking the better of it, he set course back to port when, on 21st October, the British fleet intercepted him. The French and Spanish fleet totalled 33 ships, the British had 27, but ship for ship the British had the advantage in seamanship, speed, rate and accuracy of fire and the morale and strength of the crews. Knowing this, Nelson spent little time in forming up his ships in tidy lines of battle.

Two ragged columns, in light winds with a heavy swell, and holding their fire, approached the combined fleet, one led by the *Victory* and one by Collingwood in the *Royal Sovereign*. The British ships slowly cut into the long, dispersed line of French and Spanish ships. The *Victory* took heavy casualties on the upper deck as the ships approached: 20 men were killed and 30 wounded before she fired a shot. Collingwood, by contrast, ensured that his upper deck crew lay down on the deck and avoided the worst. Twenty minutes after

Painting by Arthur William Devis of Nelson dying aboard the Victory

the *Royal Sovereign* started firing the action became general.

At 1.15pm Nelson was hit in the shoulder by a musket fired from high in the mizzen top of the French flagship, the *Redoubtable*. He knew immediately that it was fatal. Carried down below to be attended by the surgeon, he lived for about three hours, then suffered a painful death. Before he died, he knew that a great victory had been gained. The British lost no ships, either in the battle, or in the fierce storm that followed, though they had 1,700 casualties. Only 11 French and Spanish ships returned safely to Cadiz, and four escaped though they were captured soon after. Their killed and wounded amounted to 5,000, and approximately the same number were taken prisoner.

Though an overwhelming victory, Trafalgar was, from the British point of view, far from being a perfect battle; some of the heavier British ships had hardly engaged the enemy and the distribution of casualties was very uneven: after the battle there was bad feeling between captains and crews of ships which had been heavily engaged and those which had hung back. However, Collingwood made it clear to his captains that there was to be no bickering and no board of enquiry was held. As one junior officer put it: "So great was the joy of all the people of England and remaining Admiral, that all was hushed up."[*]

It was not Trafalgar which saved Britain from invasion, for nearly two months before the battle, Napoleon had realised that he could not get the temporary sea control of the Channel necessary for his invasion barges to reach English shores. On 26th August 1805 he had given orders to the "Army of England" at Boulogne to break camp and march eastwards towards Austria. Napoleon's dominance on land was not only unshaken but it increased. A day before Trafalgar, he won a battle at Ulm over the Austrians, who, ten days later, lost another at Caldiero in Italy. On 2nd December he achieved his most brilliant victory at Austerlitz over a combined Russian-Austrian army, which neutra-

[*]   Duffy, 'All was hushed up', 236

lised both these countries.

However, Trafalgar dealt the French navy a second huge psychological blow after that of the Nile. The superiority of the British was emphasised a fortnight later when a squadron commanded by Sir Richard Strachan succeeded in capturing four French ships which had escaped from Trafalgar after a four-day chase. Three months after that Admiral John Thomas Duckworth had a resounding victory at San Domingo in the West Indies. Some squadrons of large French ships continued to put to sea, but they invariably returned to port having achieved nothing.

The naval war thus took a new turn in the ten years after Trafalgar. Fleet actions became a rarity. Napoleon was still determined to invade Britain and kept on building very large ships in Antwerp, Brest and Toulon, but he ran out of skilled labour, sufficiently seasoned timber and money. In response, the British kept their ships of the line in reserve and built some new ones, considerably bigger than the *Victory*, but only one of them needed to be commissioned.

For the British, hostilities now became a question of blockade, patrols and convoys to keep trade flowing, and at the same time to deny the use of the sea to the enemy. To do this, Britain built a new, small-ship navy and the expense and intensity of the naval war increased: by 1813 there were 147,000 seamen in the navy, more than at any time in the previous 20 years. Convoys ensured the great success of the British fleet in the Baltic between 1808 and 1812, and in keeping trade flowing so that naval stores reached England to support the shipbuilding effort. The supplies of troops, equipment and provisions which kept Wellington's army in the field in the Peninsula were likewise made certain by convoys.

Thus the final and most important result of Trafalgar, which consolidated the fleet victories of Cape St Vincent and Camperdown in 1797 and the Nile in 1798, was that no fleet could challenge the British command of the ocean. Before the battle, Britain had ships of the line measuring a total of 330,000 tons, the equivalent of French, Spanish

NELSON'S FUNERAL

Cuthbert Collingwood's dispatch, written the day after the battle, reached the Admiralty on 6th November 1805. Five days later the King approved a state funeral for Nelson. In spite of the victory, the news of Nelson's death left the country muted and sombre. The mood was to darken further on 29th December when the news of Napoleon's crushing victory at Austerlitz reached London.

On 6th December the battered *Victory* reached Spithead. Nelson's body was transferred from the cask of spirits in which it had been transported to a lead coffin, which was eventually placed into the coffin made from the main mast of the *L'Orient*, the French flagship which had blown up at the Nile. The *Victory* then sailed slowly round to the Nore, where she was met by a small Admiralty yacht, the *Chatham*, which took the coffin up the Thames. Tilbury and Gravesend forts and Dutch ships combined. At Trafalgar and immediately afterwards, Spain and France lost 23 battleships, measuring almost 70,000 tons: by the end of 1805, Britain had the advantage of 570,000 tons to 350,000 tons. Britain never lost that great lead. In 1790 Britain had possessed 30 per cent of the world's ships of the line: by 1815 it was 50 per cent. It was the only time in the history of wooden navies that a single country owned half the world's battle fleet.

This fleet enabled Britain to extend her domination of the seas. In 1793 Britain had owned 26 colonies; in 1816 that figure was 43. By 1814 Britain had a worldwide network of 14 naval

---

lowered their flags, and fired minute guns. Church bells tolled.

Nelson's coffin lay in state in the Painted Hall in Greenwich Hospital for three days between 5th and 7th January 1806. Tens of thousands filed past the body. Soldiers had to be called to keep order. On 8th January the coffin was taken upriver by a state barge in a great procession to the Admiralty, where it was held for the night, and on the following day was transported in a great funeral car from the Admiralty to St. Paul's. Many remarked upon the respectful silence which hung over the large number of spectators.

It was a cold day and a very long service. Though the King was absent, all the royal Dukes were there, but Lord St Vincent pleaded illness. At the end of the service, the coffin was lowered into the crypt and interred in a magnificent tomb which had originally been made for Cardinal Wolsey, where it still rests. Within a fortnight, the war had taken the toll of another man who had not reached fifty. The Prime Minister, William Pitt, exhausted by the war, died on 23rd January. ■

bases and was in possession of the greatest and safest harbours of the world. Nelson's battles had laid the foundation of this power.

Conclusion

Nelson unquestionably symbolised a patriotic manliness to his contemporaries, and it was a grateful nation which buried him in St. Paul's Cathedral.[*] Yet inevitably the interpretation of his life has altered as attitudes and outlooks have changed over the years. We are now a long way from the certainties of a time when Great Britain was in possession of world naval supremacy with a large empire to defend.

Doubts and nuances abound as to what Nelson's memory signifies in the 20th and 21st century. He means different things to different people. For some Italian historians, he is a symbol of feudalism and oppression: at the bicentenary of the revolution in Naples in 1999, at a seminar in Portsmouth, he was called a butcher who had left "an indelible stain" on the country. Professor Antonio Gargano went so far as to call Nelson "a war criminal" on BBC radio.[**] The British professor, Andrew Lambert, however, remains confident of Nelson's heroic status: "In a secular age he remains an inspiration, tangible proof that mankind can

[*]   Wilson, 'Nelson and the People', 49-52
[**] Coleman, Nelson, 215, 350

achieve immortality".[*]

Nelson's achievement was all the greater because of his resilience. He suffered ill health, amputation and loss of sight, as well as recurrent symptoms of malaria after he had been infected during his early service. Because of the slow speed and unreliability of communications, and the consequent lack of news and of changes of government policy, very large responsibilities lay for long periods on the shoulders of fleet commanders on distant stations. In the 20th century, Nelson would have been brought home for rest. Admirals then did not generally give up their commands willingly, however, since when they were relieved they would forego prize money. Yet Nelson's exhaustion is evident: he badgered the Admiralty to get home early from both the Baltic and his Channel command in 1801; and he was beginning to ask for home leave after the strain of 18 months blockading the French in Toulon between 1803 and the beginning of 1805. If he had gone home, he would have missed Trafalgar.

It is difficult to predict how the next generation of Nelson biographies will turn out. But perhaps the most notable difference in recent years has been the change of attitude to ordinary seamen and soldiers, about whom we know so much more through the work of genealogists and their databases. Few took any notice of ordinary seamen

[*]   Lambert, *Britannia's God of War*, 361

at the time – Nelson was unusual when he mentioned an ordinary seaman by name in his dispatch from the battle of Cape St Vincent. It was an attitude which slowly began to change from the middle of the 19th century, in particular because of the suffering that was reported by war correspondents in the Crimean War. Ordinary seamen are now being given much more credit. Naval tradition was finally broken at dinner on board the *Victory* on 21st October 2005 given by the Navy Board. Her Majesty the Queen proposed the toast to Nelson, "The Immortal Memory", and added "and to those who died with him".

BIBLIOGRAPHY

Clarke, James Stanier and John M'Arthur, *The Life of
Admiral Lord Nelson K.B. from His Lordship's
Manuscripts* 2. vols. T. Cadell and W. Davies, 1809.
*A large, early deferential compendium, responsible for
many myths.*

Coleman, Terry, *Nelson: the Man and the Legend*
Bloomsbury, 2001.
*A skilful, revisionist biography; Coleman strengthened his
criticism of Nelson's decisions at Naples in the paperback
which appeared in 2002.*

Connelly, Mark, 'Trafalgar: Back on the Map of British
Popular Culture? Assessing the 2005 Bicentenary' in
Holger Hoock, *History, Commemoration and National
Preoccupation: Trafalgar, 1805-2005.* Published for the
British Academy by Oxford University Press 2007,
83-102.
A cultural assessment of the 2005 Trafalgar anniversary.

Czisnik, Marianne, *Horatio Nelson: A Controversial Hero*
Hodder Arnold, 2005.
*A rigorous scholarly treatment of Nelson's legacy, including
an analysis of French, German and Spanish authors who*

have written on Nelson.

Duffy, Michael, '"All was hushed up": the Hidden Trafalgar', *Mariner's Mirror* , 91, 2005, 216-240.
A detailed analysis of ships' logs and personal papers, demonstrating that some delayed coming into action.

Fraser, Flora, *Beloved Emma: the Life of Emma Lady Hamilton.* Weidenfeld and Nicolson, 1986.
A still-fresh, sympathetic account.

Hattendorf, John B., 'Nelson Afloat: A Hero Among the World's Navies' in David Cannadine ed., *Admiral Lord Nelson: Context and Legacy.* Palgrave Macmillan, 2005, 166-192.
An account of how much Nelson's leadership is admired in other navies.

Knight, Jane, 'Nelson and the Bronte Estate', *Trafalgar Chronicle*, 15, 2005, 133-144.
Shows Nelson's financial rewards from Bronte were greater than was supposed.

Knight, Roger, *The Pursuit of Victory: the Life and Achievement of Horatio Nelson.* Allen Lane, Penguin, 2005; *L'Amiral Nelson*, Presses Universitaires du Septentrion, 2015.
The basis for this study guide.

Britain Against Napoleon: the Organization of Victory, 1793-1815. Allen Lane, Penguin, 2013.
Explains how British naval superiority was achieved.

Lambert, Andrew, *Nelson: Britannia's God of War.* Faber & Faber, 2004.

*Written with an Edwardian certainty, allowing no doubt
about the correctness of Nelson's actions at all times.*

Mackenzie, John, 'Nelson Goes Global: the Nelson Myth in
Britain and Beyond', in David Cannadine ed. *Admiral Lord
Nelson: Context and Legacy.* Palgrave Macmillan, 2005,
144-165.
Traces the worldwide cultural memory of Nelson.

Mahan, Alfred Thayer, *The Life of Nelson: the
Embodiment of the Sea Power of Great Britain.* London,
Sampson Low, Marston & Company, 1899.
*The most influential and readable of the Victorian
biographies.*

Minto, Countess of, *Life and Letters of Sir Gilbert Elliot,
First Earl of Minto, from 1751 to 1806,* 3 vols. Longmans,
Green & Co, 1874.
Shrewd observations of Nelson throughout his career.

Morrison, Alfred, *The Collection of Autograph Letter and
Historical Documents formed by Alfred Morrison*, 2 vols.
printed for private circulation, 1894.
An essential collection of Nelson letters.

Naish, George P. B., *Nelson's Letter to his Wife and Other
Documents, 1785-1831.* Routledge and Kegan Paul, 1958.
*A scholarly and dependable collection of Nelson's letters,
largely compiled by Katherine Lindsay-MacDougall of the
National Maritime Museum.*

Nicolas, Sir Nicholas Harris, *The Dispatches and Letters
of Vice-Admiral Lord Nelson,* 7 vols. Henry Colburn, 1846
repr. Chatham Publishing, 1996.
The central collection of published Nelson letters.

Oman, Carola, *Nelson* Hodder & Stoughton, 1947, repr.
Greenhill Books, 1996.
The best mid-20th-century biography, based on
manuscripts newly available after the Second World War.

Pocock, Tom, *Horatio Nelson.* Cassell, 1987.
Written from wide knowledge, some gained from visits to all
places of Nelsonian significance, from central America to
the Nile.

Pettigrew, Thomas, *Memoirs of the Life of Vice-Admiral*
Lord Nelson, 2 vols. T & W Boone, 1849.
The first biography to examine in detail Emma Hamilton's
role in Nelson's life.

Pratt, Michael, *Nelson's Duchy: A Sicilian Anomaly.*
Spellmount, Staplehurst, Kent 2005.
Useful for the subsequent history of Bronte.

Rodger, N.A.M., *The Command of the Ocean: A Naval*
History of Britain, 1649-1815, vol.2, Allen Lane, Penguin,
2004.
Provides essential and authoritative background to
Nelson's career.

Rodger, N.A.M., 'Nelson and the British Navy:
Seamanship, Leadership, Originality' in David Cannadine
ed. *Admiral Lord Nelson: Context and Legacy.* Palgrave
Macmillan, 2005, 7-29.
A short analysis, full of insights.

Rodger, N.A.M., 'The Significance of Trafalgar: Sea Power
and Land Power in the Anglo-French Wars' in David
Cannadine ed. *Trafalgar in History: a Battle and its*
Afterlife. Palgrave Macmillan, 2006, 78-89.

Essential for context.

Southey, Robert, *The Life of Nelson* John Murray, 1813.
*The most influential of Nelson biographies, in print
continuously since it was written.*

Sugden, John, *Nelson: A Dream of Glory, 1758-1797,*
Jonathan Cape, 2004; *Nelson: the Sword of Albion.* The
Bodley Head, 2012.
*The longest and most detailed of any study of the life of
Nelson, with many insights resulting from prodigious
research.*

White, Colin, *Nelson: The New Letters* Boydell Press,
2005.
Reproduces five hundred hitherto unpublished letters.

Wilson, Kathleen, 'Nelson and the People: Manliness,
Patriotism and Body Politics' in David Cannadine ed.
Admiral Lord Nelson: Context and Legacy. Palgrave
Macmillan 2005, 49-66.
An authoritative cultural analysis.

A SHORT CHRONOLOGY

1758
29 September: Born at Burnham Thorpe, Norfolk

1771
24 April: As midshipman, joins his first ship, the
Raisonable

1777
9 April: Passes lieutenant's examination

1779
1 January: Receives commission and takes command of
the *Badger* at Port Royal, his first independent command

1783
3 July: Put on half pay, recovers from illness

1784
18 March: Appointed to command the *Boreas* cruising in
the West Indies

1787
11 March: Marries Frances Nisbet on the island of Nevis
30 November: *Boreas* paid off at Sheerness

1787-1793: On half-pay, lives in Norfolk

1793
6 January: Appointed to the *Agamemnon*
24 June: Arrives in Mediterranean

1794
18-21: Takes part in the Siege of Calvi, Corsica; loses the
sight of his right eye

1795
13-14 March: Takes part in Hotham's First Action with the
French Mediterranean Fleet
8-14 July: Takes part in Hotham's Second Action

1796
9 April: Appointed commodore

1797
14 February: Battle of Cape St Vincent
2 April: Appointed rear-admiral
25 July: Second unsuccessful attack on Santa Cruz,
Tenerife; wounded in the right arm which is amputated
27 September: Invested as Knight of the Bath

1798
1-2 August: Battle of Aboukir Bay (The Nile)
6 October: Made a baron

1799
25 June: Fleet commanded by Nelson arrives in Naples
Bay
30 June: Neapolitan Admiral Caracciolo hanged
1 August – 6 November: Journey across Europe and North
Sea with the Hamiltons

1801

January: Appointed vice-admiral

January: Separates from Fanny Nelson

29 January : Birth of Horatia to Emma

2 April: Battle of Copenhagen

5 May – 19 June: Commander-in-chief, Baltic

15 May: Made a viscount

24 July: Commands anti-invasion force in Channel

4-5 August: Squadron bombards Boulogne

16 August: Second attack on Boulogne

23 October: Strikes his flag for 'Admiralty leave'

24 October: Purchases Merton Place

1802

21 July – 5 September: Tour with the Hamiltons to Wales

1803

16 May: Appointed commander-in-chief, Mediterranean

19 May: Hoists flag on board the *Victory*

8 July: Takes command off Toulon

1805

11 May – 3 June: Passage of the Mediterranean fleet
across the Atlantic in pursuit of the Franco-Spanish Fleet

14 June – 18 July: British fleet returns to Gibraltar

18 August 14 September: Returns to England

29 September: Takes command of the fleet off Cadiz

21 October: Battle of Trafalgar; Nelson killed

INDEX

ℭℊ CONNELL GUIDES

MORE IN OUR NEW HISTORY SERIES

Guides
The French Revolution
Winston Churchill
World War One
The Third Reich
Stalin
Lenin
Nelson
Napoleon
The Cold War
The American Civil War
The Normans

Russia and its Rulers
The Amerian Civil Rights
Movement

Short Guides
Britain after World War Two
Edward VI
Mary I
The General Strike
The Suffragettes
President Truman
President Lincoln

"Connell Guides should be required reading in every school in the country."
Julian Fellowes, creator of Downton Abbey

"What Connell Guides do is bring immediacy and clarity: brevity with depth. They unlock the complex and offer students an entry route."
Colin Hall, Head of Holland Park School

"These guides are a godsend. I'm so glad I found them."
Jessica Enthoven, A Level student, St Mary's Calne

"Completely brilliant. I wish I were young again with these by my side. It like being in a room with marvellous tutors. You can't really afford to be without them, and they are a joy to read."
Joanna Lumley

To buy any of these guides, or for more information, go to
www.connellguides.com
Or contact us on (020)79932644 / info@connellguides.com

LITERATURE GUIDES

Novels and poetry
Emma
Far From the Madding Crowd
Frankenstein
Great Expectations
Hard Times
Heart of Darkness
Jane Eyre
Lord of the Flies
Mansfield Park
Middlemarch
Mrs Dalloway
Paradise Lost
Persuasion
Pride and Prejudice
Tess of the D'Urbervilles
The Canterbury Tales
The Great Gatsby
The Poetry of Robert Browning
The Waste Land
To Kill A Mockingbird
Wuthering Heights

Shakespeare
A Midsummer Night's Dream
Antony and Cleopatra
Hamlet
Julius Caesar

King Lear
Macbeth
Othello
Romeo and Juliet
The Second Tetralogy
The Tempest
Twelfth Night

Modern texts
A Doll's House
A Room with a View
A Streetcar Named Desire
An Inspector Calls
Animal Farm
Atonement
Beloved
Birdsong
Hullabaloo
Never Let Me Go
Of Mice and Men
Rebecca
Spies
The Bloody Chamber
The Catcher in the Rye
The History Boys
The Road
Vernon God Little
Waiting for Godot

NEW
A Short History of English
Literature
American literature
Dystopian literature

How to read a poem
How to read Shakespeare
The Gothic
The poetry of Christina Rossetti
Women in literature

First published in 2017 by
Connell Guides
Spye Arch House
Spye Park
Lacock
Wiltshire
SN15 2PR

10 9 8 7 6 5 4 3 2 1

A CIP catalogue record for this book is available from the British Library.

ISBN 978-1-911187-46-2

Design © Nathan Burton

Assistant Editors:
Brian Scrivener and Paul Woodward

Printed in Great Britain

www.connellguides.com